Play for Me, Peter

Written by

Carol Selick

Illustrations by Blueberry Illustrations

Find Our Books at Amazon, Barnes & Noble, IngramSpark & More!

Children's Books & Music can be found at: www.CarolSelickBooks.com

www.SlothDreamsBooks.com

Peter would never forget the day he heard Grandpa Henry play the piano.

His hands jumped and his foot thumped and Peter felt the music from his head to his toes.

"I want to play just like Grandpa."

"When he plays, I have to move," Grandma told Peter. Then she danced with him all around the room.

Grandpa Henry was a jazz musician. He played
piano in nightclubs, restaurants, and concert halls.

JAZZ!!!! Peter liked the way it sounded.

One Saturday, Grandpa taught Peter a song,
"Heart and Soul". Peter learned the melody
and Grandpa played the chords.

"We're jamming," he told Peter.

But then the music stopped. The piano sat in the corner looking sad. Grandma looked sad, too.

Grandpa was gone.

"He's still playing his music in heaven.
Play for me, Peter. The house is too quiet."

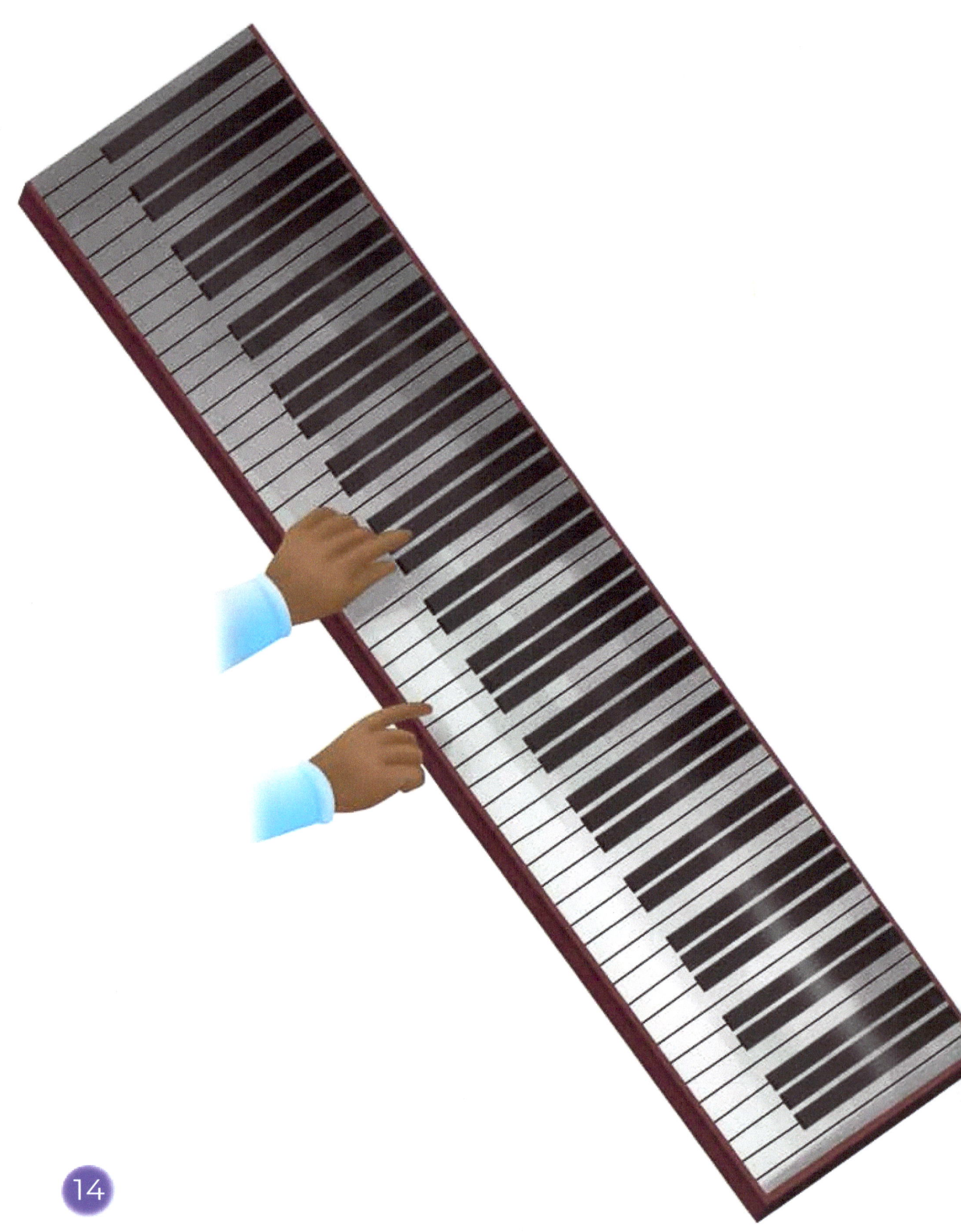

"Heart and Soul" didn't sound the same
without his duet partner.

"Let me try another song."

He pressed the white keys, PLINK!!!!
He pressed the black keys, KERPLUNK!!!!

Peter opened the piano bench
stuffed with sheet music.

He stared at the black dots.
He studied the squiggly lines.

Peter lifted a pile of music, and an envelope fell
to the floor.

"What's this? It has my name on it!"

"Open it," Grandma said.

The envelope was filled with money.

"That's where Grandpa hid his money! It's his
gift to you. I know what he'd want us to do with
it. Let's go for a drive."

Grandma parked in front of a music store.

"Look at all the pianos!" Peter shouted.

"I'm Mr. Wally," said the man behind the counter. "Do you want to learn to play the piano?"

"Yes! I want to play just like my grandpa!"

They walked to a small room at the back of the
store, just big enough for a piano.

"This is Middle C. Put your right thumb on Middle
C and curve your fingers on the keys, Peter."

Mr. Wally pointed to the upper lines in the piano
book.

"The sounds get higher and higher like climbing a
ladder. Repeat after me:"

"Every, Good, Boy, Does, Fine!"

Peter pressed his fingers on the keys and played his first song.

"That didn't sound like the jazz music my grandfather played."

"You mean like this?" Mr. Wally's fingers raced up and down the keyboard.

"That's what I'm talking about!"

"You can play like that if you practice and work hard. It's going to take time."

Every day after school, Peter went to
Grandma's house to practice his lessons.

He played through the seasons –
Winter, Spring, Summer, and Fall.

BACH
BEETHOVEN
Boogie
WOOGIE BLUES

He played simple songs, and then harder songs.

He practiced scales and finger exercises and songs by famous composers like Bach and Beethoven.

He even played Boogie Woogie and jazz music.

One day Grandma said, "Keep playing! You've got the same magic that Grandpa had! He would be so proud of you! When you play, I can't sit still!"

Then she got up and danced all around the room.

Every Good Boy Does Fine

— Carol Selick

About the Author

Carol Selick is a music educator with a degree in Early Childhood and Elementary Education from Rutgers University.

Carol is a performing singer and songwriter and co-founded and directed the New Jersey

Children's Opry where she wrote and performed original songs.

Her recordings, *Life Is Believing in You and Just Gonna Think About Today*, feature a mix of standards and originals. Carol is also the author of an award-winning coming-of-age book, "Beyond the Song" which is based on her early years in the music business.